Reading DoodleLoops

Creative Whole Language Activities for Beginning Readers

written and illustrated by
Sandy Baker

Copyright © 1994, Good Apple

ISBN No. 0-86653-791-0

Printing No. 987654

Good Apple
A Division of Frank Schaffer Publications, Inc.
23740 Hawthorne Boulevard
Torrance, CA 90505-5927

Acknowledgment

My deepest thanks to Donna Napolitano, devoted professional, for her encouragement and continual support.

Published by Good Apple © 1994, Sandy Baker

A Word About *Reading DoodleLoops*

The DoodleLoops included in this book are a unique learning tool! They offer a meaningful and stimulating way to introduce and/or practice letter sounds and skills. Reading DoodleLoops are simply short descriptions of characters and/or scenes which the children must illustrate. Each DoodleLoop emphasizes a specific letter sound (such as short vowels), combinations of letter sounds (such as long vowels, blends, digraphs), and compound words—the basic language skills taught at the primary grade levels.

For example, if the children are learning or practicing the short *a* sound, the directions may read:

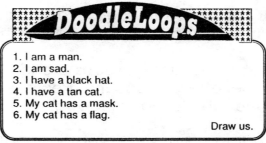

DoodleLoops

1. I am a man.
2. I am sad.
3. I have a black hat.
4. I have a tan cat.
5. My cat has a mask.
6. My cat has a flag.

Draw us.

Watch your students' language skills and reading comprehension skills improve as they read to follow directions in order to create their own unique, creative illustrations.

How to Use *Reading DoodleLoops*

1. As you introduce or want to reinforce a specific letter sound or skill (such as short vowels, long vowels, blends, etc.), use the corresponding DoodleLoops. The skill being featured is noted at the bottom of each page.

2. The first time the children are asked to complete a Reading DoodleLoop, distribute a copy to each child.

   a. Read the directions to the class or have the children read them out loud.

   b. You may wish to illustrate one page on the board or overhead projector, or have a student illustrate it. For example:

(This is a sample illustration for the short *a* DoodleLoop shown above.)

Published by Good Apple © 1994. Sandy Baker

GA1485

c. Then ask the children to illustrate their own copies.

*d. Optional: Brainstorm a list of other words containing the same letter sound(s) or skill that you are teaching. Tell the children that they may add any of these words to their illustrations.

For example, using the sample short *a* page from page iii, the children could add any of the following to their pictures: an apple, a bat, an astronaut, a rabbit, bags, a rat, and so on.

3. Promote creativity. Encourage the children to use color; make their illustrations vivid, detailed, and clear; and use their imaginations.

4. After the first few Reading DoodleLoops are introduced to the group, it should no longer be necessary to read the directions orally. The children should be asked to follow the directions on their own.

a. Emphasize the importance of reading *all* of the directions before illustrating. It helps even more to read them at least twice before starting to draw.

b. Remind the children to enhance their drawings by adding illustrations of other words that contain the letter sound(s) or skill being taught.

5. You may also allow the children to create their own DoodleLoops using the blank DoodleLoop on page 90. Emphasize that they incorporate a specific skill or letter sound(s) into their directions.

6. You may also wish to have the children find the specific letters, sounds, or skills being emphasized on the DoodleLoops. They may then underline or circle them.

a. For example, if you are emphasizing compound words on a page, the children can underline all compound words and draw a line between the two words in each, such as:
I am a <u>cow|boy</u>.

b. For example, if you are emphasizing soft *c* on another page, the children can underline or circle all *c*'s which make the *s* sound, such as:
Ⓒyrus ate Ⓒelery.

The Importance of Sharing

1. It is essential that the children have a vehicle for sharing their DoodleLoops in order to reinforce their ideas, to have support and feedback from their classmates, and to encourage divergent thinking.

Published by Good Apple © 1994, Sandy Baker

GA1485

2. The children may share their work in a variety of ways. You may choose one or more of the following:

Daily Sharing: Share the DoodleLoops as a group. If time allows, each child may share his or her DoodleLoop with the class. If not, four or five children may share daily so that over the course of a week, all of the children have had one turn to share.

Bulletin Boards: Display some of the more complex and creative DoodleLoops on a special bulletin board, or if space allows, display all of the children's DoodleLoops.

Overhead Transparencies: Each day you may wish to have one child make an overhead transparency of the DoodleLoop. After the other children in the group have completed their DoodleLoops, you can share the overhead with the class.

Sharing with Another Class: You may wish to have your class or a group of your students share their DoodleLoops with another classroom.

Evaluation

1. Reading DoodleLoops give a good indication of the development of the children's phonetic skills.

2. Reading DoodleLoops give a good indication of the level of the children's comprehension skills.

3. Reading DoodleLoops give a good indication of the children's ability to follow directions.

Family Involvement

1. When the DoodleLoops are first introduced, it is helpful to write a letter to each child's family explaining their purpose. A sample letter is provided on page vi.

2. It is very important that the children share their DoodleLoops with their families. They provide a wonderful connection between school and home, and families truly enjoy sharing with their children and watching their progress over the course of the year.

Enjoy DoodleLoops!
They offer endless possibilities for learning
and for expanding creative awareness!

Published by Good Apple © 1994, Sandy Baker

GA1485

Dear Family,

This year your child will be working on some very special pages called Reading DoodleLoops.

Reading DoodleLoops present children with an enjoyable way to learn, practice, and reinforce their reading skills. They also serve as an excellent tool for following directions and improving reading comprehension.

Each DoodleLoop provides a short description of a character or scene which the children must illustrate. Each DoodleLoop also incorporates a specific letter sound(s) (such as short *a* or long *i*) or skill (such as compound words) into the directions. The children must be able to read the words in order to follow the directions and properly illustrate the characters and scenes. Therefore, the children are learning and/or practicing letter sounds and reading skills in the context of the directions.

The following is a sample Reading DoodleLoop emphasizing the short *a* sound:

The skill emphasized on each page will always be indicated at the bottom of the page.

Please take time to discuss and share these special pages with your child. They serve as a wonderful tool to teach, reinforce, and enrich reading and comprehension skills, as well as enhance creativity.

Thank you so much for your cooperation, involvement, and support.

Sincerely,

Published by Good Apple © 1994, Sandy Baker

GA1485

DoodleLoops

1. I am a man.
2. I am sad.
3. I have a black hat.
4. I have a tan cat.
5. My cat has a mask.
6. My cat has a flag.

Draw us.

Short a

Published by Good Apple © 1994, Sandy Baker

GA1485

DoodleLoops

1. I am Jan.
2. I am with Sam.
3. Our dad is with us.
4. We are at camp.
5. We all have backpacks.

Draw us.

Short a

Published by Good Apple © 1994, Sandy Baker

GA1485

DoodleLoops

1. We are Dan, Pam, and Brad.
2. We are in a band.
3. Brad is fat.
4. Pam is a brat.
5. Dan is glad.
6. The fans clap their hands.

Draw us.

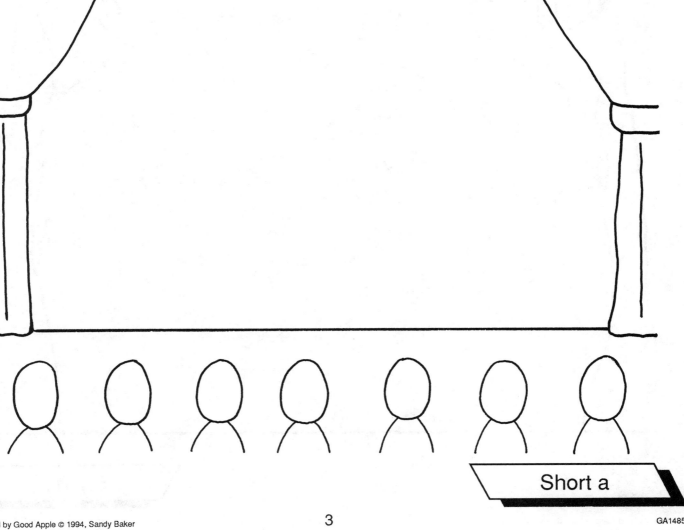

Short a

Published by Good Apple © 1994, Sandy Baker

GA1485

1. I am a witch.
2. I have big lips.
3. I have a wig.
4. My sister is with me.
5. We have six pigs.

Draw us.

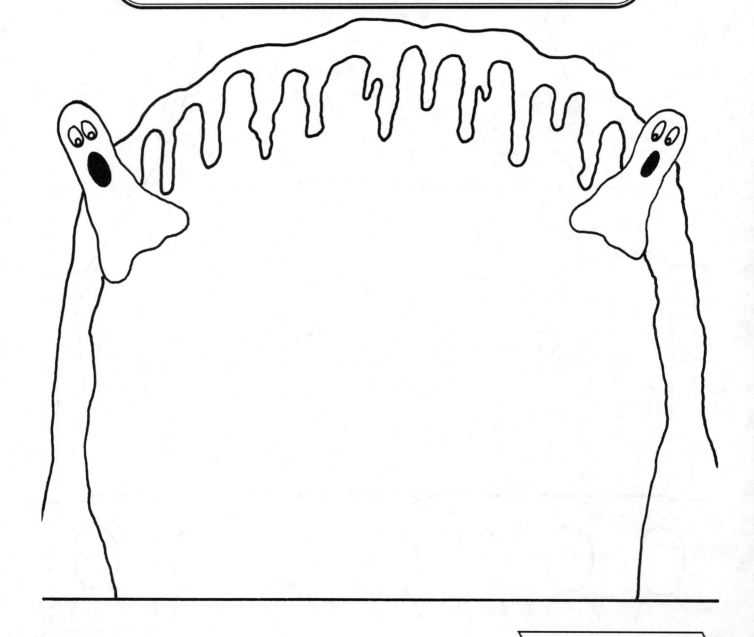

Short i

1. I am Jill.
2. I live in an igloo.
3. I have mittens on.
4. I am with my friend Liz.
5. We have ribs for dinner.
6. We have bibs.

Draw us.

Short i

Published by Good Apple © 1994, Sandy Baker

DoodleLoops

1. We are Bill and Jim.
2. We are kids.
3. We are twins.
4. We are on a hill.
5. We have twin hippos with us.

Draw us.

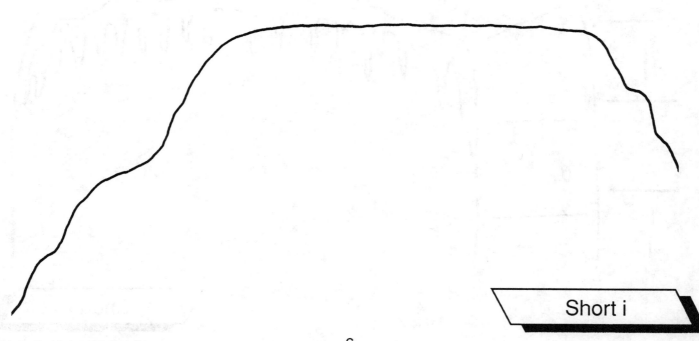

Short i

Published by Good Apple © 1994, Sandy Baker

GA1485

DoodleLoops

1. I am Pat.
2. I can do tricks.
3. I have a magic kit.
4. I can grab a rabbit from my hat.
5. My hat is black.
6. The rabbit is fat.

Draw me.

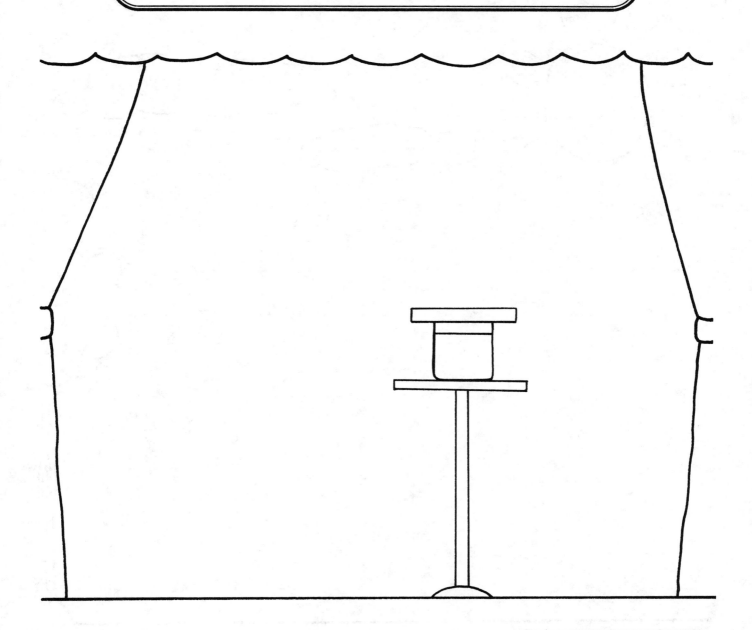

Short a and i

Published by Good Apple © 1994, Sandy Baker

GA1485

DoodleLoops

1. I am a bug.
2. I am funny.
3. I am in the sun.
4. I have a drum.
5. I am with a skunk and a duck.

Draw us.

Short u

Published by Good Apple © 1994, Sandy Baker

GA1485

DoodleLoops

1. I am Jud.
2. I am with Russ.
3. We are on the bus.
4. We have gum.
5. We can make bubbles.

Draw us.

STOP

Short u

Published by Good Apple © 1994, Sandy Baker

GA1485

DoodleLoops

1. We are Gus and Bud.
2. We have umbrellas.
3. We play in a puddle.
4. We have a pup named Fluff.
5. Fluff is stuck in the mud.

Draw us.

1. I am Pat.
2. I was bad!
3. I had jam on my lap.
4. It stuck on my slacks.
5. I jumped up!
6. I dumped the jam on the rug!

Draw me.

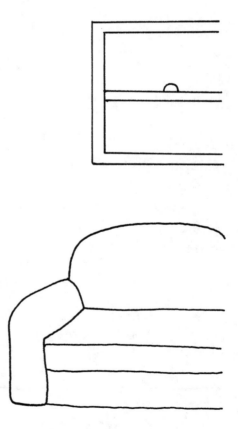

Short a and u

DoodleLoops

1. I am Ron.
2. I am with my mom.
3. We like to jog.
4. We are hot.
5. We have dots on our socks.

Draw us.

Short o

Published by Good Apple © 1994, Sandy Baker

GA1485

DoodleLoops

1. I am Tom.
2. I am with my pop.
3. I have the chicken pox.
4. I went to the Doc.
5. I am on a cot.

Draw us.

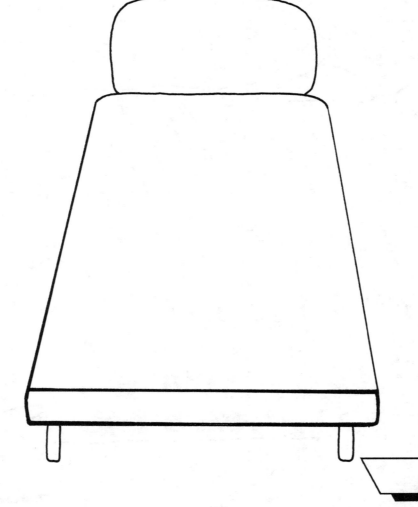

Short o

Published by Good Apple © 1994, Sandy Baker

GA1485

DoodleLoops

1. We are three red blobs.
2. We live in a pond.
3. We have lots of spots.
4. There are rocks by the pond.
5. A green glob is on the rocks.

Draw us.

Short o

Published by Good Apple © 1994, Sandy Baker

GA1485

DoodleLoops

1. I am Jack.
2. I am with Jon.
3. We stack lots of blocks.
4. Nan and Bob are with us.
5. They play tag.

Draw us.

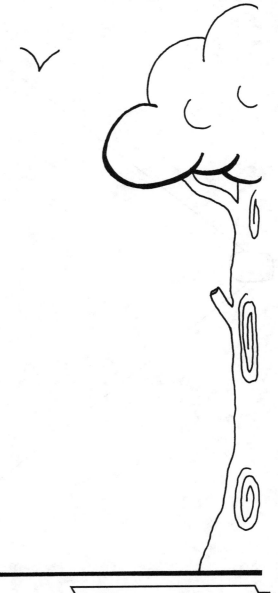

Short a and o

Published by Good Apple © 1994, Sandy Baker

GA1485

DoodleLoops

1. I am on the White Sox.
2. The pitcher has a mitt.
3. I just made a hit.
4. I slid in!
5. We have got to win!

Draw me.

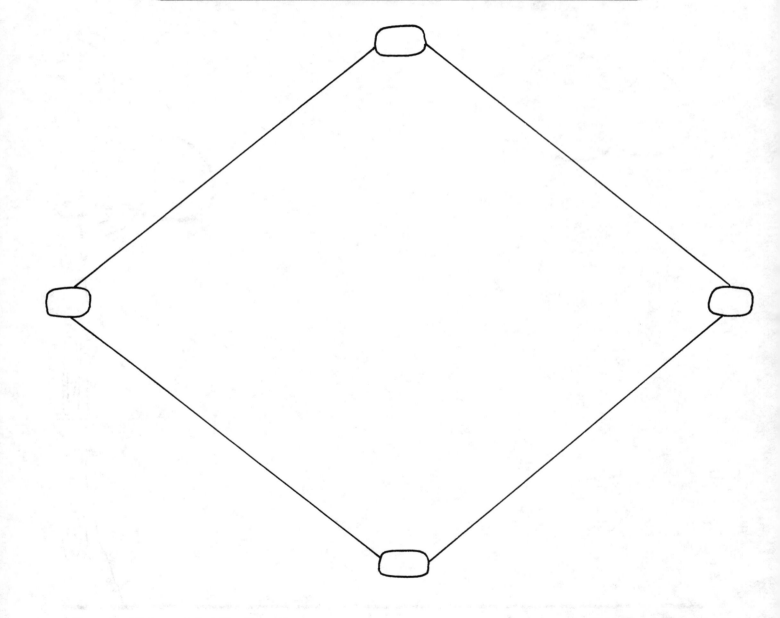

Short i and o

Published by Good Apple © 1994, Sandy Baker

GA1485

1. We are three kids.
2. We are Tad and Bob and Jill.
3. We are with our mom and dad.
4. We are fishing.
5. We have fishing rods.
6. Dad has a big, fat fish on his rod!

Draw us.

Short a, i, and o

GA1485

1. Bob is a slob.
2. His mom had a fit!
3. He has lots of junk.
4. He must pick it up.
5. He has a big job!

Draw Bob and his mom.

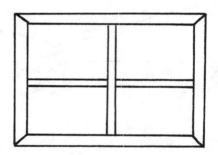

Short i, o, and u

DoodleLoops

1. We are four bugs.
2. We are black.
3. Two of us have big dots.
4. Two of us have little dots.
5. We are jumping on the rug.

Draw us.

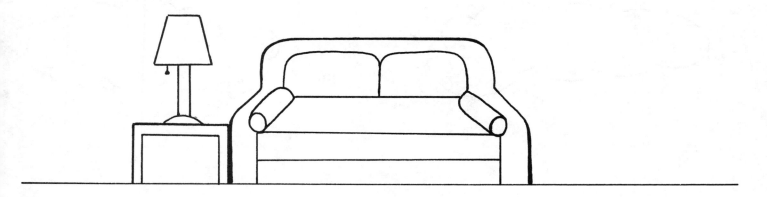

Short a, i, o, and u

DoodleLoops

1. I am Meg.
2. I have a red dress.
3. Fred is my friend.
4. Fred has a hen.
5. The hen is yellow.
6. The hen is in a nest.

Draw us.

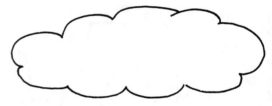

Short e

1. I am Ken.
2. I am at my desk.
3. I have a pen.
4. I am taking a test.
5. Peg is next to me at her desk.

Draw us.

$$\begin{array}{r} 2 \\ + 2 \\ \hline \end{array}$$ $$\begin{array}{r} 3 \\ + 6 \\ \hline \end{array}$$

A B C D
E F G H

Short e

Published by Good Apple © 1994, Sandy Baker   GA1485

DoodleLoops

1. I am Ben.
2. I am a vet.
3. I have a vest.
4. I have a pet in a net.
5. The pet has ten legs.

Draw us.

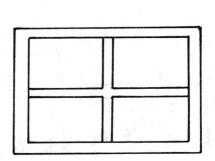

Dr. Bark
Vet

Short e

DoodleLoops

1. Tad and Nell ran fast.
2. Tad and Nell fell.
3. Tad is mad.
4. Nell is a mess.
5. Ted and Ned will yell!

Draw them.

Short a and e

Published by Good Apple © 1994, Sandy Baker

GA1485

DoodleLoops

1. I am Jen.
2. I am sick.
3. I am in bed.
4. I must rest.
5. I have red Jell-O™.

Draw me.

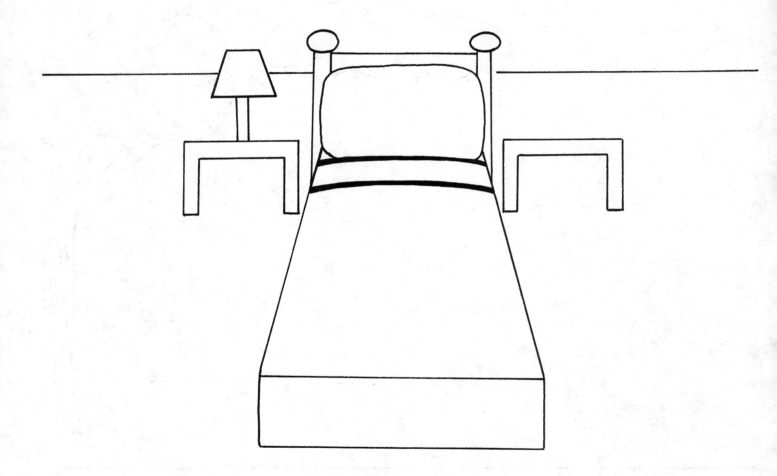

Short e and i

Published by Good Apple © 1994, Sandy Baker

GA1485

1. Mick got a gift.
2. It is a doctor's kit.
3. His friend Fred is ill.
4. Fred asks Mick for help.
5. Mick will help Fred get well.

Draw them.

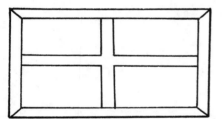

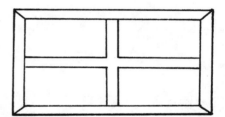

Short a, e, and i

Published by Good Apple © 1994, Sandy Baker
GA1485

1. We are Liz and Greg.
2. We are in the desert.
3. The sun is hot.
4. We are on camels.
5. We are on the sand.
6. We have two tents.

Draw us.

Short a, e, i, o , and u

DoodleLoops

1. My name is Nate.
2. I have skates on.
3. I have a cape.
4. I am with my snake.
5. We are in space.

Draw us.

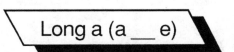

Long a (a ___ e)

Published by Good Apple © 1994, Sandy Baker

GA1485

DoodleLoops

1. We are Ray and Kay.
2. We are playing with clay.
3. The clay is gray.
4. We have a pet blue jay.
5. The jay has a crayon.

Draw us.

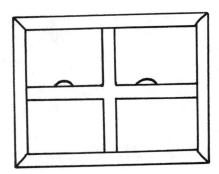

Long a (ay)

DoodleLoops

1. My name is Gail.
2. I have braids.
3. I have painted nails.
4. I am in the rain.
5. I can see a rainbow.

Draw me.

Long a (ai)

Published by Good Apple © 1994, Sandy Baker

GA1485

DoodleLoops

1. We are Jane and Gail.
2. We are sailing on the lake.
3. It is raining.
4. There are big waves.
5. A whale came by.

Draw us.

Long a (review)

GA1485

1. I am Mike.
2. I am riding on my bike.
3. I am flying a kite.
4. My kite has stripes.
5. My five white mice are with me.

Draw us.

Long i (i __ e)

DoodleLoops

1. I am on a flight.
2. It is night.
3. We are flying high.
4. I see a bright light.
5. What a sight!

Draw what I see.

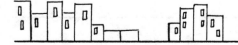

Long i (igh)

Published by Good Apple © 1994, Sandy Baker

GA1485

DoodleLoops

1. Hi! I am going to dine.
2. I have a wide tie.
3. I am with my wife.
4. She is sitting to my right.
5. We are eating pie.
6. We each have a slice.

Draw us.

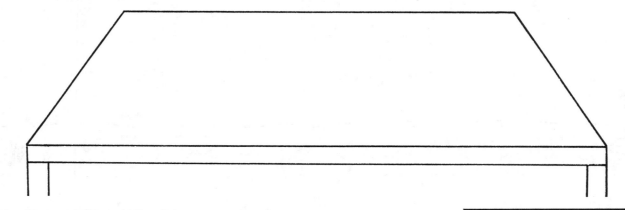

Long i (review)

DoodleLoops

1. I am June.
2. I am cute.
3. I am on a huge mule.
4. I am playing a tune on my flute.
5. I am with my friend Luke.

Draw us.

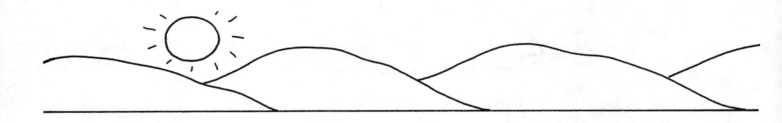

Long u (u __ e)

Published by Good Apple © 1994, Sandy Baker

GA1485

1. I am Sue.
2. I am on a cruise.
3. I am eating fruit.
4. I am with my friend June.
5. June is drinking juice.

Draw us.

Long u (ue, ui, u ___ e)

Published by Good Apple © 1994, Sandy Baker

GA1485

DoodleLoops

1. I am Joan.
2. I am on a boat.
3. My pet toad is with me.
4. My pet goat is with me too.
5. We all have coats.

Draw us.

Long o (oa)

Published by Good Apple © 1994, Sandy Baker

GA1485

1. I am Rose.
2. I am on the phone.
3. I am wearing a robe.
4. I am eating a cone.
5. I am standing by the stove.

Draw me.

Rose's Kitchen

Long o (o ___ e)

Published by Good Apple © 1994, Sandy Baker

GA1485

DoodleLoops

1. I am a ghost.
2. I have a big nose.
3. It glows.
4. I have a gold coat.
5. I am holding a rose.
6. I am floating.

Draw me.

Boo!

Boo!

Long o (review)

Published by Good Apple © 1994, Sandy Baker

GA1485

DoodleLoops

1. I am a beast.
2. I am mean.
3. I have a beak.
4. I am screaming.
5. I am eating a meal.
6. I am eating meat and peas and beans.

Draw me.

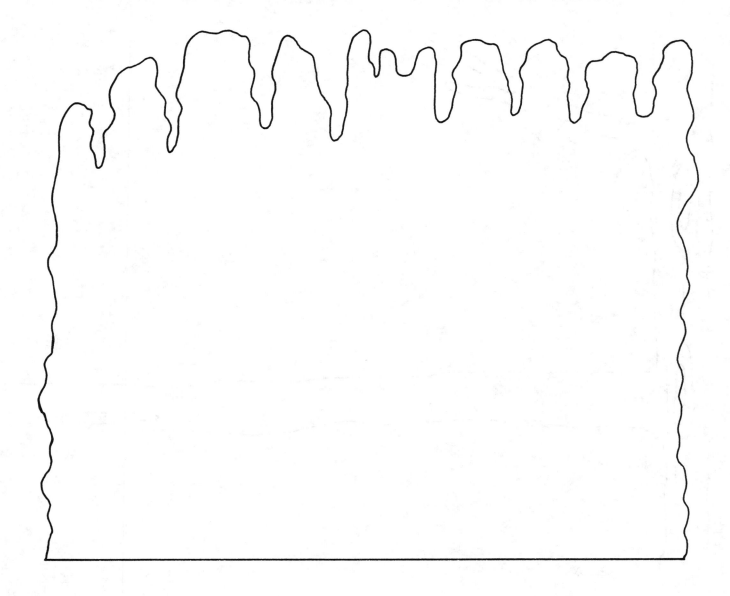

Long e (ea)

Published by Good Apple © 1994, Sandy Baker

GA1485

DoodleLoops

1. My name is Lee.
2. I am three.
3. A bee came after me.
4. I ran up a tree.
5. I see the bee on my knee!

Draw me.

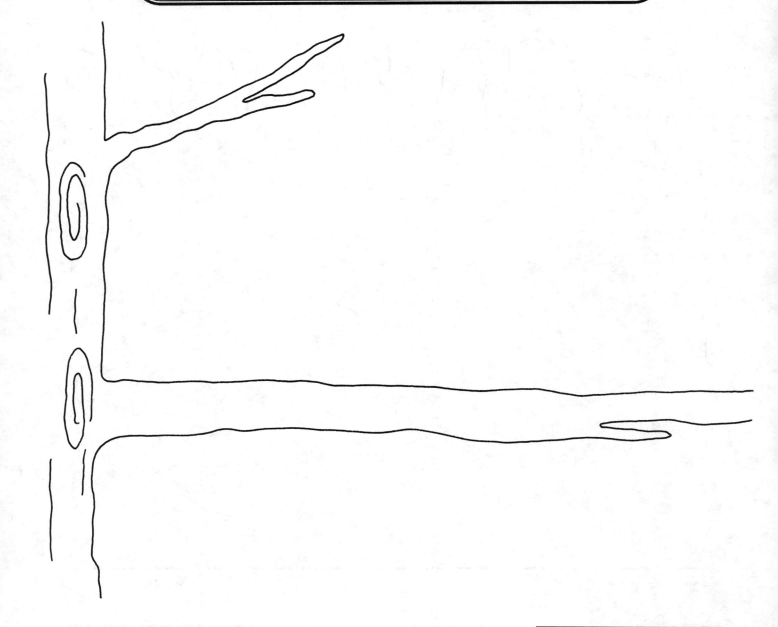

Long e (ee)

Published by Good Apple © 1994, Sandy Baker

GA1485

DoodleLoops

1. I am Pete.
2. I am sleeping.
3. I am having a creepy dream.
4. A mean creature is after me.
5. He is very near.
6. He is going to leap at me.
7. I have to scream!

Draw my dream.

Long e (review)

Published by Good Apple © 1994, Sandy Baker

GA1485

DoodleLoops

1. I am a brontosaurus.
2. I am with my bride.
3. We are brown.
4. My bride is wearing bracelets.
5. We are baking brownies.

Draw us.

Blend br

Published by Good Apple © 1994, Sandy Baker

1. We are two creepy creatures.
2. One creature is cross-eyed and looks crazy.
3. The other creature is crying.
4. We are both cream-colored.
5. We are wearing crooked crowns.

Draw us.

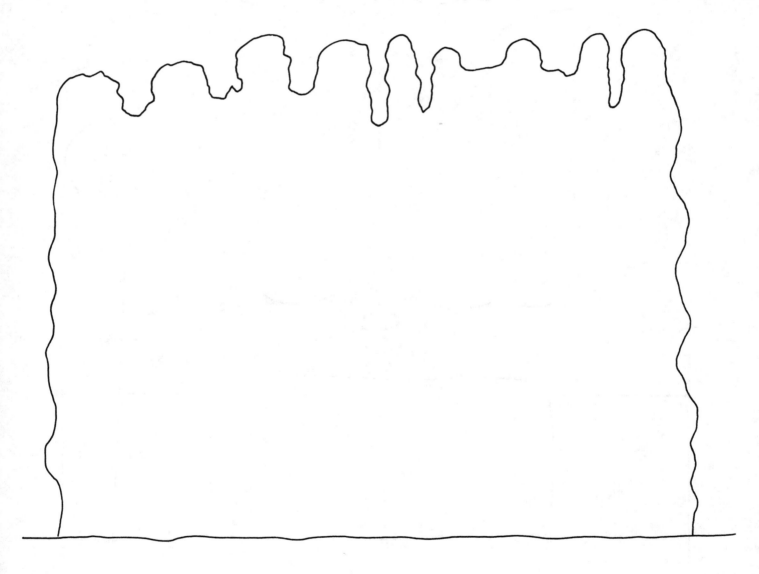

Blend cr

DoodleLoops

1. I am Drew.
2. I am dreaming.
3. My dream is about a dragon.
4. The dragon is wearing a dress.
5. The dragon is playing the drums.

Draw me and my dream.

Blend dr

GA1485

DoodleLoops

1. We are Fran and Frank.
2. We both have freckles.
3. We are with a freak.
4. The freak is Frankenstein.
5. Frankenstein is not friendly.
6. We are so frightened that we are frozen!

Draw us.

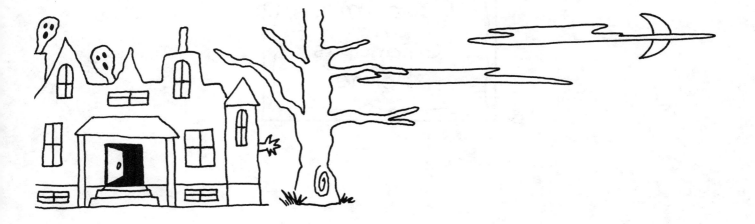

Blend fr

Published by Good Apple © 1994, Sandy Baker GA1485

1. We are Grandma and Grandpa.
2. We have gray hair.
3. We are with our granddaughter and grandson.
4. We all have green eyes.
5. We are all eating green grapes.

Draw us.

Blend gr

DoodleLoops

1. I am a prince.
2. I am eating pretzels.
3. I am with a princess.
4. The princess is pretty.
5. The princess is holding presents.

Draw us.

The Royal Palace

Blend pr

Published by Good Apple © 1994, Sandy Baker GA1485

DoodleLoops

1. My name is Troy.
2. I am a troll.
3. My hat is shaped like a triangle.
4. I live in a tremendous tree.
5. I am holding a treasure.

Draw me.

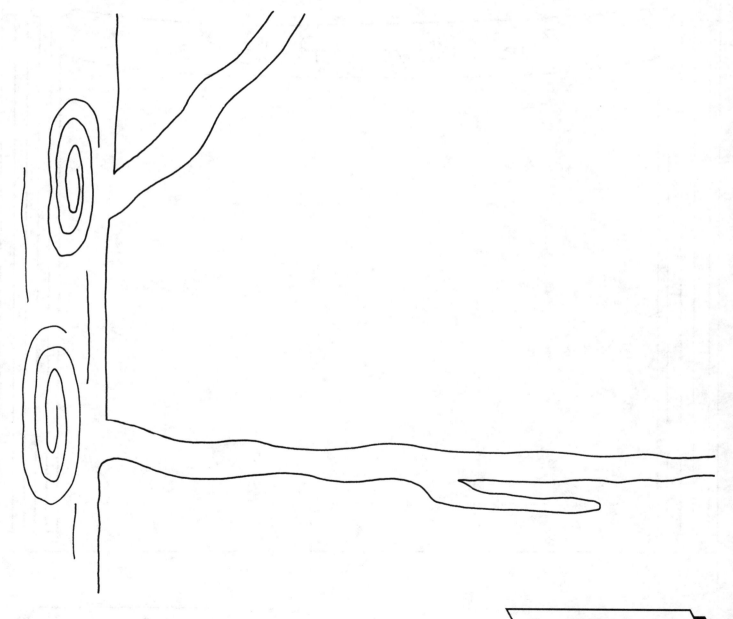

Blend tr

Published by Good Apple © 1994, Sandy Baker

GA1485

DoodleLoops

1. I am Blanch.
2. I am blond.
3. I have a blue blouse.
4. I am playing with blocks.
5. I am by a blackboard.

Draw me.

Blocks

Blend bl

Published by Good Apple © 1994, Sandy Baker

GA1485

DoodleLoops

1. I am Clyde.
2. I am a clown.
3. I am with Claudia.
4. Claudia is a clown too.
5. We are standing by our clubhouse.
6. It is cloudy.

Draw us.

Blend cl

Published by Good Apple © 1994, Sandy Baker

GA1485

DoodleLoops

1. I am Flo.
2. I live in Florida.
3. I am a florist.
4. I grow flowers.
5. I also play the flute.

Draw me.

Blend fl

Published by Good Apple © 1994, Sandy Baker

GA1485

DoodleLoops

1. I am Glenn.
2. I am with Glenda.
3. We live on a glacier.
4. We are wearing gloves.
5. We both wear glasses.

Draw us.

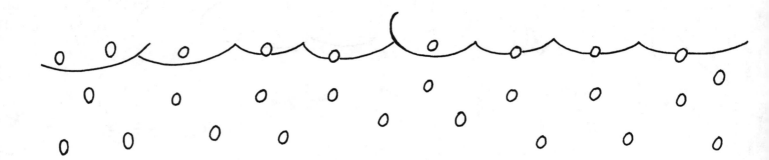

Blend gl

GA1485

DoodleLoops

1. I am a plant.
2. I live on another planet.
3. The planet is Pluto.
4. I am plum-colored.
5. I am plump, and I love to play.

Draw me.

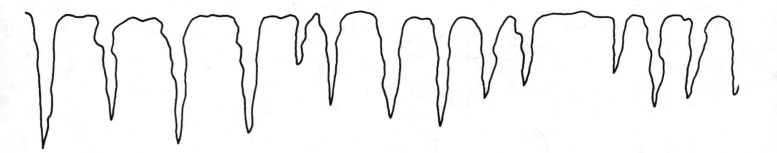

Blend pl

Published by Good Apple © 1994, Sandy Baker

GA1485

DoodleLoops

1. My name is Scott.
2. I am a scout.
3. I am riding on my scooter.
4. I see a scarecrow.
5. He is wearing a scarf.
6. He scares me!

Draw me.

Blend sc

GA1485

DoodleLoops

1. I am a skeleton.
2. I have no skin, just bones!
3. Boy! Am I skinny!
4. I am on skates.
5. I am starting to skid.

Draw me.

Blend sk

Published by Good Apple © 1994, Sandy Baker

DoodleLoops

1. My name is Mrs. Smith.
2. I am very small.
3. I always smile.
4. I am wearing a smock.
5. I smell smoke in my house!

Draw me.

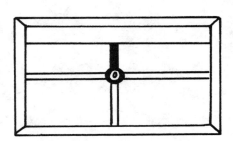

Mrs. Smith's House

Published by Good Apple © 1994, Sandy Baker

GA1485

DoodleLoops

1. I am Stanley Stupid.
2. I am very strong.
3. I am standing on my hands.
4. I am in the street.
5. It is starting to storm.
6. I hope it stops!

Draw me.

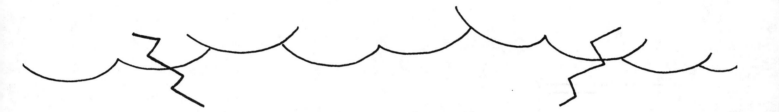

Blend st

Published by Good Apple © 1994, Sandy Baker

GA1485

DoodleLoops

1. It is time to go to sleep.
2. I take off my slippers.
3. I slide into bed.
4. I slip under the covers.
5. When I fall asleep, I start to sleepwalk.

Draw me.

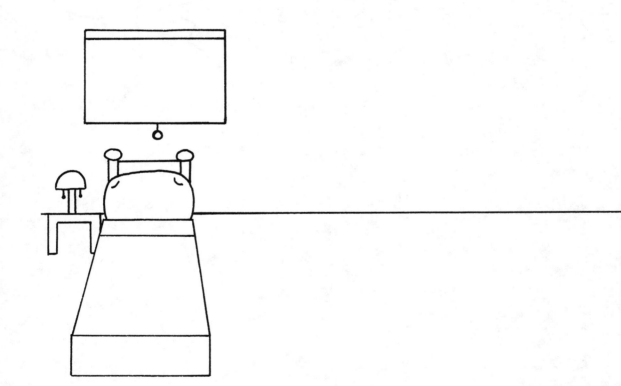

Blend sl

Published by Good Apple © 1994, Sandy Baker

GA1485

DoodleLoops

1. I am a snowman.
2. I sneak in the house.
3. I have a snack.
4. I snuggle up for a snooze.
5. I snore and snore.

Draw me.

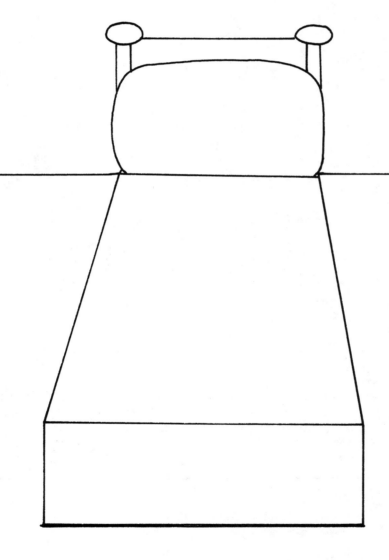

Blend sn

Published by Good Apple © 1994, Sandy Baker

GA1485

DoodleLoops

1. I look up in space.
2. A spaceship is speeding to Earth.
3. It spins, and it sparkles.
4. It is spooky.
5. I see spacemen.
6. Can they speak?

Draw what I see.

Blend sp

Published by Good Apple © 1994, Sandy Baker
GA1485

DoodleLoops

1. Today we had a swell time.
2. I played on the swings.
3. My friend went for a swim.
4. He is a swift swimmer.
5. A swan swam by.

Draw us.

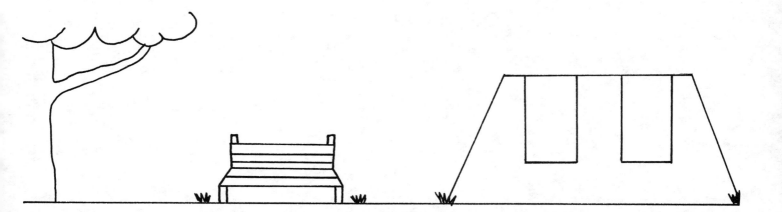

Blend sw

Published by Good Apple © 1994, Sandy Baker

GA1485

DoodleLoops

1. We are twins.
2. We are both twenty.
3. We are twelve feet tall.
4. We are outside, and it is twilight.
5. The stars are starting to twinkle.

Draw us.

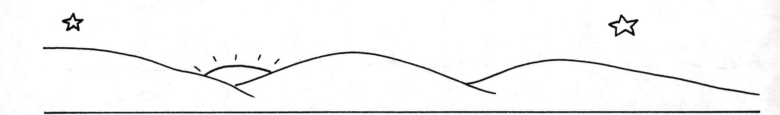

Blend tw

Published by Good Apple © 1994, Sandy Baker

GA1485

DoodleLoops

1. It is spring.
2. The sun is strong.
3. I am splashing in my sprinkler.
4. The strong spray is squirting on me.
5. I am wearing a striped bathing suit.
6. I am screaming and squealing.

Draw me.

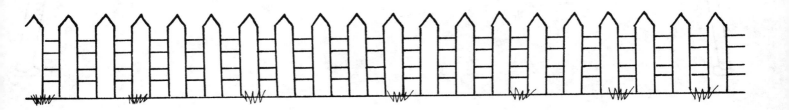

Blends scr, spl, spr, squ, and str

1. I am a king.
2. I am sitting on a swing.
3. I am wearing many rings.
4. I am singing a song.
5. It is spring.

Draw me.

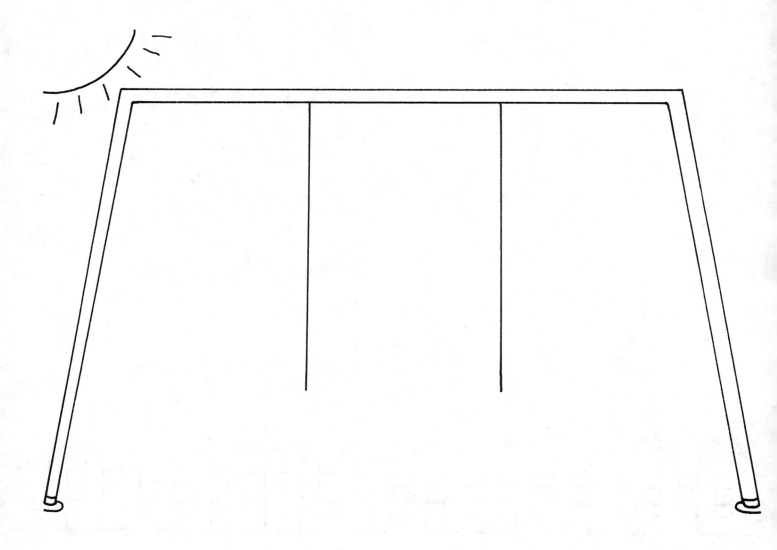

Ending ng

DoodleLoops

1. I am at camp.
2. I saw a wasp.
3. I jumped on a stump.
4. The wasp stung me.
5. Now I have a bump.
6. I feel like a grump.

Draw me.

1. I am a blond child.
2. I am with my old friend.
3. My friend is bald.
4. We like to hold hands.
5. We are standing on the sand.
6. We both play in a band.

Draw us.

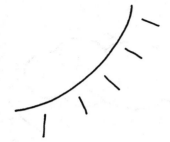

Endings nd and ld

GA1485

DoodleLoops

1. I am a beast.
2. I am having a feast.
3. I invited a guest.
4. She is my aunt.
5. She brought me a gift.
6. It is a plant that is starting to wilt.

Draw us.

Endings lt, ft, nt, and st

DoodleLoops

1. My name is Hank.
2. I am an elf.
3. I am wearing a mask.
4. I love to play golf.
5. I sank a hole in one all by myself.

Draw me.

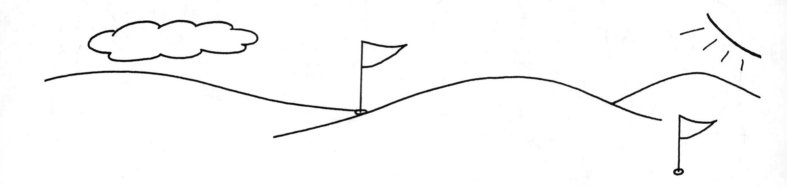

Endings lf, nk, and sk

GA1485

DoodleLoops

1. We are thirteen things.
2. We are sitting on thrones.
3. We have thorns on us.
4. We are thin.
5. We each have three thumbs.

Draw us.

Published by Good Apple © 1994, Sandy Baker

Blend th

DoodleLoops

1. I am a whale.
2. I am white.
3. I have whiskers.
4. My tail whacks the water.
5. My friend the whaler is whistling for me.

Draw us.

1485

ood Apple © 1994, Sandy Baker   GA1485

DoodleLoops

1. We are Shelly and Sherry.
2. We have shiny shoes.
3. Our shirts have shells on them.
4. We are on a ship.
5. There are sharks.

Draw us.

Blend sh

DoodleLoops

1. I am Chuck.
2. I am a child.
3. I have cherry red cheeks.
4. I am chubby.
5. My chimp is chasing me!

Draw us.

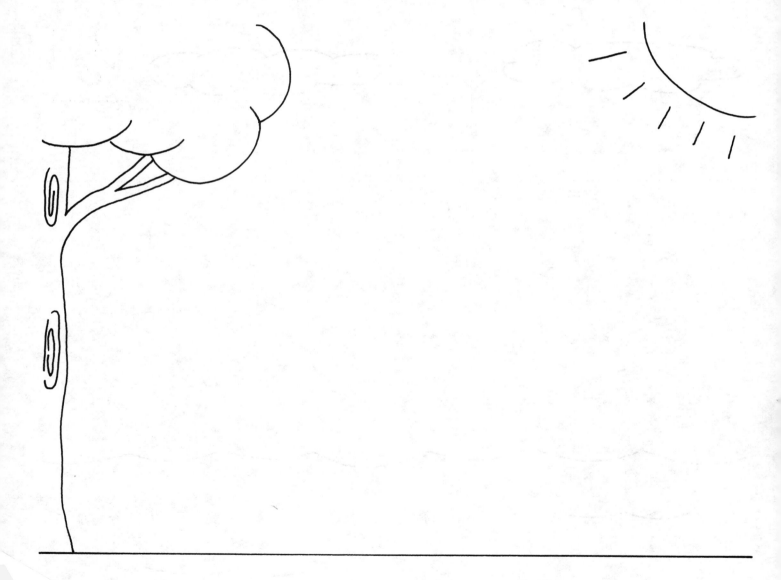

Blend ch

DoodleLoops

1. I am Chad.
2. I am a cheerleader.
3. I like to show off with my cheers.
4. I am very short.
5. I never shave.

Draw me.

| Home | 21 |
| Visitors | 0 |

DoodleLoops

1. I am Sharon.
2. I am on a white ship.
3. I can see three whales.
4. I am very thin.
5. I am eating a cheeseburger, chips, and a thick cherry shake.

Draw me.

Blends sh, ch, th, and wh

od Apple © 1994, Sandy Baker

GA1485

DoodleLoops

1. I am Roth.
2. I am in the bath.
3. I am doing math.
4. I lost a lot of teeth.
5. I have a big mouth.

Draw me.

Ending th

Published by Good Apple © 1994, Sandy Baker

DoodleLoops

1. We are Trish and Josh.
2. We have a pet fish.
3. Trish has long lashes.
4. She is washing dishes.
5. Josh is throwing out the trash.

Draw us.

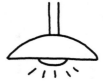

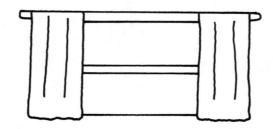

d Apple © 1994, Sandy Baker

Ending sh

DoodleLoops

1. I am a witch.
2. I am eating lunch on the beach.
3. I have a sandwich and a peach.
4. I like to munch on my lunch.
5. I am sitting on a bench.

Draw me.

Ending ch

Published by Good Apple © 1994, Sandy Baker

DoodleLoops

1. I am Beth.
2. I lost a tooth at lunch.
3. I heard a crunch.
4. I must watch for the tooth fairy.
5. I have a wish.

Draw the tooth fairy and me. What is my wish?

Endings ch, sh, and th

d Apple © 1994, Sandy Baker

DoodleLoops

1. My name is Jack.
2. My hair is thick and black.
3. I am on my deck.
4. I have lots of toy trucks.
5. I am having a snack.

Draw me.

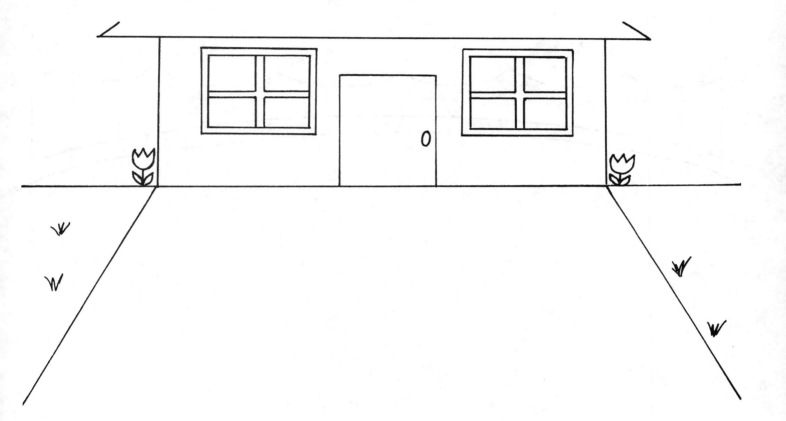

Ending ck

Published by Good Apple © 1994, Sandy Baker

DoodleLoops

1. My name is Cyrus.
2. I am in the circus.
3. I am on a cycle.
4. I am playing the cymbals.
5. I am making a face.

Draw me.

Soft c

d Apple © 1994, Sandy Baker

1. I am a prince.
2. I am with a princess.
3. We are facing a fireplace.
4. We have fancy clothes.
5. We are drinking cider.

Draw us.

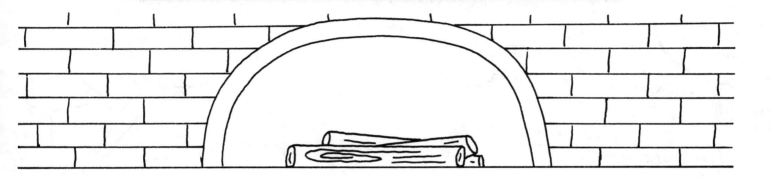

Soft c

Published by Good Apple © 1994, Sandy Baker

DoodleLoops

1. I am a giant.
2. My name is George.
3. I am wearing gym shoes.
4. I have a pet giraffe in a cage.
5. I live in a gingerbread house.

Draw me.

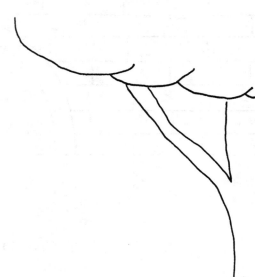

Soft g

DoodleLoops

1. I am a genie.
2. I am huge.
3. I am wearing a gem.
4. I am on a bridge.
5. I am eating vegetables.

Draw me.

Soft g

Published by Good Apple © 1994, Sandy Baker

GA1485

DoodleLoops

1. I am Sandy.
2. I am very skinny.
3. I am silly.
4. I am making a funny face.
5. My friend is Bobby.
6. Bobby is chubby.

Draw us.

y (vowel-e sound)

Published by Good Apple © 1994, Sandy Baker

GA1485

DoodleLoops

1. I am a guy.
2. I can fly.
3. I am up in the sky.
4. I want you to fly by me.
5. Can you try?

Draw you and me.

Published by Good Apple © 1994, Sandy Baker

GA1485

DoodleLoops

1. Why am I so scary?
2. I am hairy.
3. I am creepy.
4. My cry is spooky.
5. My eyes are shiny.

Draw me.

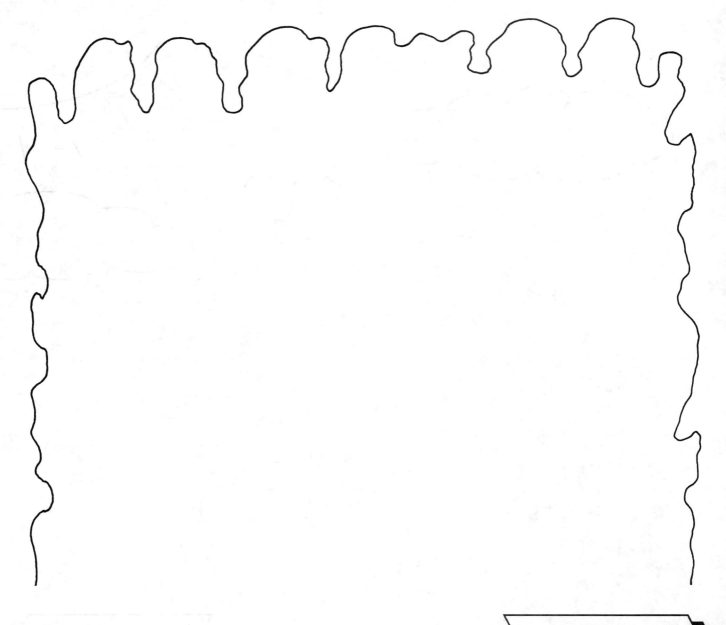

y (vowel—e and i sounds)

DoodleLoops

1. I am nineteen.
2. It is my birthday today.
3. Everyone is at my party.
4. They are eating popcorn and peanuts.
5. I have a birthday cupcake for myself.

Draw us.

Compound words

DoodleLoops

1. Everybody is playing outside.
2. They are wearing overcoats.
3. They are making snowmen.
4. They are throwing snowballs.
5. The snowflakes are falling everywhere.

Draw them.

Compound words

Published by Good Apple © 1994, Sandy Baker

GA1485

DoodleLoops

1. I am on a sailboat.
2. I am wearing a raincoat.
3. I am wearing sunglasses.
4. The sunlight is very bright.
5. I can see a rainbow.

Draw me.

Compound words

Published by Good Apple © 1994, Sandy Baker

GA1485

DoodleLoops

1.
2.
3.
4.
5.

Draw me.

Published by Good Apple © 1994, Sandy Baker

GA1485